Collins Revised

Engaging English 3

Workbook

Ruby Bose

Components of DigiSuite

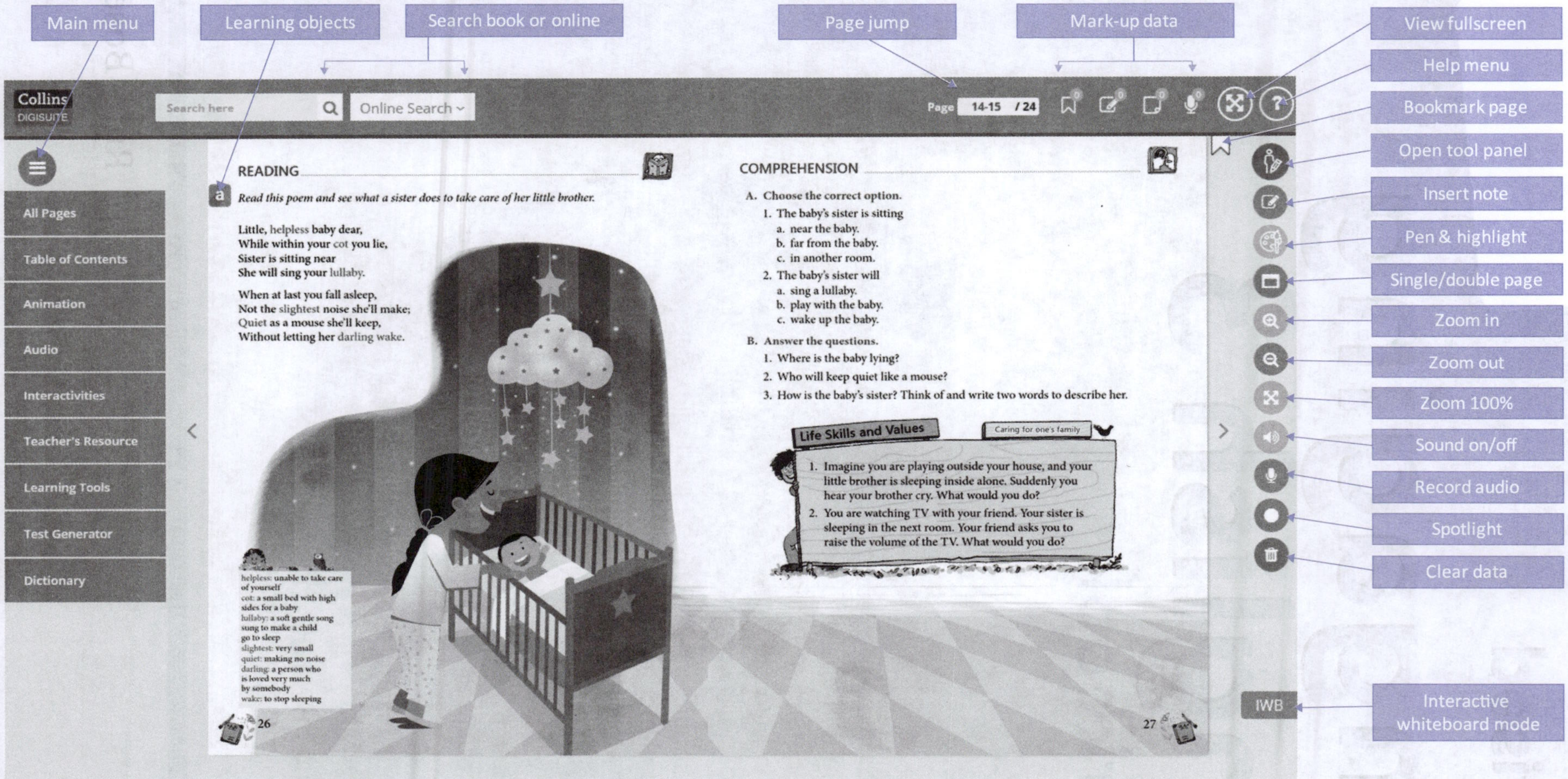

Student + Teacher			Teacher-only	
a animations	**ia** activities	**g** games	**lp** lesson plans	**tn** teacher's notes
ilt instructor-led tutorials	**w** worksheets	**v** videos	**w** worksheets	**ak** answer keys
	audio			

Preface

Revised Engaging English aims to instill an appreciation for literature in today's learners, while equipping them with the tools to develop native fluency and communicative competence in using the English language. The eight-level series comprises Coursebooks, Workbooks, and digital resources for teachers for all levels.

The revised edition has been aligned closely with the guidelines of the National Education Policy, 2020 through its focus on twenty-first century skills, Sustainable Development Goals (SDGs), cross-curricular learning, 'Happiness' content and art-integrated learning. Coursebooks and Workbooks 1 and 2 integrate the essence of NIPUN (National Initiative for Proficiency in Reading with Understanding and Numeracy). They aim to motivate students to read independently, improve their vocabulary, develop their critical thinking and creative skills and enhance their ability to express themselves verbally and in writing.

The lessons are built around carefully selected literary pieces with distinct cross-curricular themes, and presented with glossary, explanation of literary terms and interesting trivia. The end-of-chapter exercises address the needs of formal language learning.

The **Workbooks** are designed to complement the Coursebooks, by providing additional skills practice, review and assessments. They comprise the following sections:

Comprehension includes factual, inferential and evaluative questions based on short reading passages.

Way with Words includes exercises on the vocabulary topics encountered in the Coursebook as well as extension activities derived from it. It also incorporates activities on literary devices and figures of speech, spelling drills and exercises on dictionary usage.

Grammar in Use starts with a short explanation of important grammar concepts covered in the Coursebook, followed by plenty of practice for reinforcement.

Listening and Speaking builds students' oral and aural communication skills. It includes tasks such as phonics drills, conversation practice, role plays and debates to develop spoken English skills. Listening comprehension exercises teach students to listen for both general and specific details. In poetry chapters, there are activities on stress, rhyme and metre.

Pen it Down: The activities in this section include guided and free writing tasks derived from the reading text, which build on the functional and creative writing skills of the learner.

Each Workbook also contains two **Tests**. One of these is based on the principle of SAFAL (Structured Assessment For Analyzing Learning), a competency-based assessment introduced by CBSE. They assess the competencies of critical thinking as well as inquiry-based and analysis-based learning. The other test is modelled on class assessments.

The series encourages competency-based education which allows concept acquisition at the learner's own pace, based on individual ability. We hope that it will foster a love for literature and reading in young learners.

Detailed Contents

Unit	Themes	Way with Words	Grammar in Use	Listening and Speaking	Pen it Down
1. A Glass of Milk	Neighbourhood and Community	• Word meanings • Anagrams	• Adjectives • Material nouns • Nouns: gender	• Completing a dialogue and enacting a conversation	• Diary writing
2. A Faithful Act	Friendship and Loyalty	• Word search: describing words • Binomial pairs	• Collective nouns • Personal pronouns	• Listening and choosing; expressing one's opinion	• Paragraph writing
3. The Rooks	A Home of One's Own	• Words with multiple meanings • Names of birds (crossword)	• Tenses: simple past, present and future • Verbs	• Listening to a process and giving instructions	• Paragraph writing
4. Holiday Activities	India's Northeast	• Using *to/too/two* • Words related to travel	• Prepositions of time and place • Comparison of adjectives	• Talking about holiday activities • Different pronunciation of words ending in *-ed*	• Completing a paragraph
5. The History of Chocolate	Food Around the World	• Homophones • Crossword on chocolate • Contextual words and phrases	• Question words • Conjunctions	• Listening comprehension • Explaining a process	• Picture composition
6. The Elf and the Dormouse	Folktales	• Word search: fantasy creatures • Expressions	• Common and proper nouns • Inverted commas	• Reciting a poem and identifying rhyming words	• Paragraph writing
7. The Seed of Truth	Tales from India	• Proverbs • Using suffixes: *-ful*, *-tion*	• Types of sentences • Indefinite and definite articles	• Listening to a passage for details and stating true/false • Narrating a story	• Paragraph writing
8. Breakfast	Health and Nutrition	• Compound words related to food • Words related to smell	• Agreement of subject and verb • Conditional sentences using *if*	• Having a class discussion and stating if information is true or false	• Making lists

Unit	Themes	Way with Words	Grammar in Use	Listening and Speaking	Pen it Down
9. Adventure at the Circus	Family and Friends	• Synonyms of *eat* • Movement words	• Adverb-verb collocation • Forming adverbs from adjectives	• Listening and identifying /*sh*/ or /*s*/ sound in words • Asking and giving permission	• Paragraph writing
Test Paper					
10. Two Little Kittens	Our Pets	• Rhyming words • Using prefixes: *un-*, *dis-*, *in-*, *im-*	• Contractions • Negative sentences with *not*	• Participating in a conversation and resolving an argument	• Writing an apology letter
11. Anna's Experiments with Weather	Women in Science	• Homophones • Collocations	• Subject and predicate • Possessive and demonstrative pronouns	• Listening to an announcement and answering questions	• Making a list of emergency items
12. Kangaroos	Animals from Down Under	• Words with multiple meanings	• Verb and object • Negative contractions: *can't*, *couldn't*, *won't* and *wouldn't*	• Pronunciation: long and short *i* sound	• Drawing and paragraph writing
13. Amparo's Journey	Brave Deeds	• Synonyms of *scared* • Word forms: nouns and verbs	• Prepositional phrases • Present continuous tense	• Spinning a story yarn	• Picture composition
14. The Land of Fib	Space Stories	• Homophones • Jumbled words	• Helping verbs • Past continuous tense • Using *and*	• Listening to a story and answering questions	• Writing a letter of thanks
15. The Land of Counterpane	Physical Activities and Sports	• Contextual words and phrases • Classification • Making sentences	• Modal verbs • Types of adjectives	• Pronunciation: long and short *e* sounds in words spelled with *ea*	• Paragraph writing
16. Emily's Brush with History	Ancient History	• Using suffixes: *-ness*, *-ful*, *-dom* • Contextual words	• Joining sentences using *who* • Punctuation	• Identifying the silent letter	• Writing a letter
17. An Animal's Prayer	Saving the Environment	• Similes • Crossword	• Using apostrophes	• Describing a picture	• Making a poster
Assessment (SAFAL)					

Contents

1
A Glass of Milk

Way with Words

Word Meanings

A. Complete the sentences with the correct words from the brackets.

1. Please do not __________ in the corridor. (walk/run)
2. We should not __________ out the answers in the class. (shout/speak)
3. The nut was so __________ that Fatima could not crack it open. (difficult/hard)
4. If you want good results, you need to __________ regularly. (examine/study)
5. The children __________ amongst themselves. (fought/struggled)
6. There were so many flies that the food had to be __________. (filled/covered)
7. Mira wore a beautiful __________ dress to the party. (new/fresh)
8. The milk is __________. Please drink it after some time. (hot/burning)
9. The children wanted __________ toffees. (most/more)
10. I will __________ you a snack. (buy/by)

Anagrams

An **anagram** is a word that is made by rearranging the letters of another word.
Example: **bat → tab**

B. Rearrange the letters of the following words to create new words.

1. cat __________
2. arc __________
3. night __________
4. save __________
5. state __________
6. chin __________
7. dusty __________
8. listen __________
9. care __________
10. knee __________

Grammar in Use

ADJECTIVES

You know that **adjectives** are describing words. **Example:** The **kind** girl fed him.

A. Complete the sentences with suitable adjectives.

1. The rose is a ____________ flower.
2. My mother was ill because of a ____________ headache.
3. The box was so ____________ that Rian could not lift it.
4. We could not see anything because of the ____________ rain.
5. Dr Bernard was a ____________ and ____________ man.
6. We should not eat ____________ food.
7. I am reading an ____________ book. It has many ____________ pictures.
8. My teacher is very ____________ to us.

MATERIAL NOUNS

Material nouns are names of materials from which things are made. **Example:** sugar

B. Read these sentences and underline the material nouns.

1. My mother is wearing bangles made of gold.
2. Can you pass me the salt?
3. This statue is made of glass.
4. Ramesh's shop sells bags made of jute.
5. Children should drink milk every day.
6. We cannot live without water.
7. The honey in that jar is mine.
8. I bought a saree made of cotton for my sister.

NOUNS: GENDER

C. Rewrite the sentences by changing the gender of the underlined nouns.

1. The king and the prince rewarded the soldiers.

   ____

2. The mother went with her daughter to the market.

   ____

3. The wizard was chasing the peacock in the forest.

   ____

4. The emperor and the nobleman entered the church together.

   ____

5. The landlord asked the actor to pay the rent.

____

6. We spotted some deer and a lion in the jungle.

____

Listening and Speaking

Work with a partner and fill in the blanks asking for his help. Then, enact the conversation with your partner.

Raju: Why didn't you join us for the cricket match?

Ramu: I was in bed for a week as ____________________.

Raju: How are ____________________?

Ramu: Much better. But, I have a small problem.

Raju: ______________________________?

Ramu: I have to complete the English project work using information from the Internet, but I don't have ____________________ at home.

Raju: You can come to my house and use ____________________ to find the ____________________.

Ramu: ____________________. You are very kind.

Pen it Down

You had an unexpected visitor last weekend, with whom you had a wonderful time. You look forward to more such experiences. Write a diary entry using the given words and phrases.

wonderful time	enjoyable weekend	made a scrapbook
baked a cake	looked at photo albums	went for a walk
surprise visit	favourite person	created great memories

Dear Diary, Date: ____________

____

____

____

____

2
A Faithful Act

Comprehension

Read the passage and answer the questions.

A ship sank during a storm at sea. Only two men were able to save themselves and swim to a small island. Both were good friends. They agreed that they had no other option but to pray to God. However, to find out whose prayer was more powerful, they decided to divide the area between them and stay on opposite sides of the island.

The first thing they decided to pray for was food. The next morning, the first man saw a tree with fruits on his side of the land, and he was able to eat its fruit. The other man's portion of land remained barren.

Soon the first man prayed for a house, clothes and more food. The next day, like magic, all of these were given to him. However, the second man still had nothing.

Finally, the first man prayed for a ship, so that he could leave the island. In the morning, he found a ship waiting in the sea beyond the beach on his side of the island. The first man boarded the ship and decided to leave the second man behind.

As the first man was about to leave, he heard a voice from heaven, 'Why are you leaving your friend behind?'

'My blessings are mine alone, since I was the one who prayed for them,' the first man answered. 'My friend's prayers were all unanswered and so he does not deserve anything.'

'You are mistaken!' the voice said. 'He had only one prayer, which I answered. If not for that, you would not have received any of my blessings.'

The first man asked the voice, 'What did he pray for that I should owe him anything?'

'He prayed that all your prayers be answered.'

A. Complete the sentences using words from the passage.

1. The ship sank in a __________.
2. The two survivors were able to swim to a __________.
3. The first thing they prayed for was __________.
4. The first man wanted to leave the island, so he prayed for a __________.
5. When the first man was about to leave, he heard a voice from __________.

B. Arrange the sentences in the order of events in the passage.

1. The first man boarded the ship. ☐
2. The two men swam to an island. ☐
3. The first man heard a voice when he was about to leave. ☐
4. The first man asked for a house, clothes and more food. ☐
5. The first man decided to leave the second man behind. ☐

C. Read the line from the passage and answer the questions.

1. *'He had only one prayer, which I answered.'*

a. Who said these words and to whom?

____

b. Whom does 'he' refer to?

____

c. What was the only prayer that the person being spoken about have?

____

____

d. What does this tell us about the person being spoken about?

____

____

D. According to you, what happened at the end of the story? Complete the story in a few lines.

____

____

____

____

____

____

____

Way with Words

Words Related to Birds

A. Find six adjectives in the word grid that can be used to describe the crow.

A	B	C	D	E	F	G	H	I	H	J	K	L
M	N	O	P	Q	R	S	T	U	O	V	W	X
B	L	A	C	K	Y	Z	A	B	O	C	D	G
E	F	G	H	I	J	C	K	L	D	M	N	L
S	T	O	U	T	O	A	P	Q	E	R	S	O
T	U	V	W	X	Y	R	Z	A	D	B	C	S
D	E	F	G	H	I	R	J	K	L	M	N	S
I	N	T	E	L	L	I	G	E	N	T	O	Y
P	Q	R	S	T	U	O	V	W	X	Y	Z	A
B	S	C	A	V	E	N	G	E	R	C	D	E

Binomial Pairs

A **binomial pair** is a set of two words joined by a conjunction. It is used to show a relationship between the two words.

Example: safe and sound

B. Match the words in column A with those in column C using the options given in column B. One is done for you.

Column A	Column B	Column C
1. bits		a. later
2. more		b. lose
3. pick	and	c. pieces
4. sooner		d. wide
5. far	or	e. less
6. win		f. choose

Grammar in Use

Collective Nouns

A **collective noun** is used to talk about the number of persons or things that are grouped together and are thought to be a whole.

Example: a **murder** of crows

A. Complete the sentences with suitable collective nouns from the box.

board	range	flock	team	herd	galaxy

1. I saw a __________ of stars through the telescope.
2. The driver stopped his car as a __________ of deer was crossing the road.
3. We saw a __________ of mountains from the window of the room.
4. The __________ of directors had a meeting to finalise the project.

5. The captain successfully led his __________ of players to win the match.
6. A __________ of sheep was grazing in the field.

Personal Pronouns

A **personal pronoun** is used to replace the name of a person, animal or thing in a sentence.

Example: The cook had two plates in his hands. **He** dropped **them** in surprise.

B. Complete the paragraph with personal pronouns.

My name is Radha and ________ am an Indian. My mother is a professor and ________ teaches in a college. My father is a pilot and ________ is often away from home for months. My grandparents live with ________. ________ are very kind and loving. I love ________ a lot. ________ often go on holidays together. When my father is at home, ________ plays with my younger brother and ________.

Listening and Speaking

Listen carefully to the two situations and choose a situation that shows the child has behaved in the right way. Share with your partner reasons to support your choice.

Pen it Down

In the story, you read about the way the commander crow was faithful to his king. Write a paragraph describing an incident in which you were faithful to someone.

You may include these points:

- who was the person you were faithful to
- what was the incident
- did you get a reward or words of appreciation
- what was the reward or how were you praised

3
The Rooks

Way with Words

Words with Multiple Meanings

Some words can have two or more meanings.
Example: The word **crane** has three meanings.
- a type of bird
- a type of machine
- to stretch out to see something

A. Find two different meanings of the given words and make sentences with them.

1. **arm**
   a. meaning: ____________________
   sentence: ____________________
   b. meaning: ____________________
   sentence: ____________________

2. **row**
   a. meaning: ____________________
   sentence: ____________________
   b. meaning: ____________________
   sentence: ____________________

3. **slip**
   a. meaning: ____________________
   sentence: ____________________
   b. meaning: ____________________
   sentence: ____________________

Names of Birds

B. Read the clues and complete this crossword puzzle. The number of letters is given in brackets.

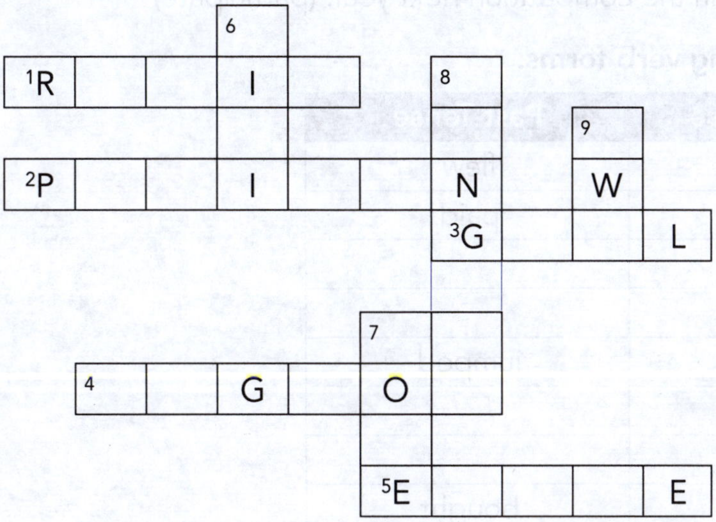

Across

1. a small bird, with a red chest (5)
2. a large water bird with a long beak (7)
3. a water bird with long pointed wings and short legs (4)
4. a bird used as a messenger (6)
5. large, powerful bird of prey (5)

Down

6. a flightless bird, found in New Zealand (4)
7. a bird that stands for peace and love (4)
8. a black and white coloured flightless bird living mostly in Antarctica (7)
9. a bird with large eyes which makes a hooting sound (3)

Grammar in Use

Tenses

The **simple present tense** is used to show an action that is taking place at the present moment, to talk about a habit and to express a universal truth.

The **simple past tense** is used to show an action that has been completed in the past.

The **simple future tense** is used to show an action that will take place in the future.

A. Fill in the blanks with the correct form of the verbs given in brackets.

1. Ravi __________ a certificate for reading with expression. (receive)
2. The president of the club __________ the village next week. (visit)
3. When air becomes hot, it __________. (rise)
4. Two years ago, I __________ Pune. (leave)

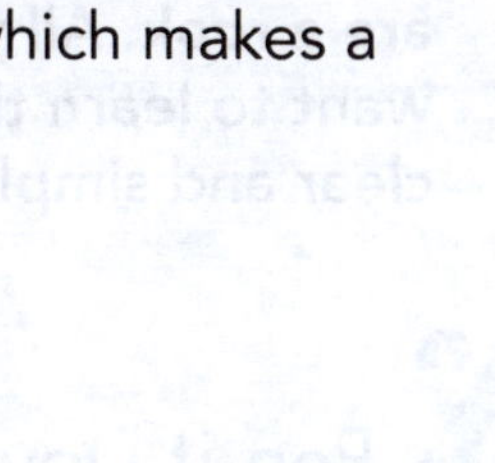

5. My uncle __________ all the work on his own. (do)

6. I __________ in the competition next year. (participate)

B. Write the missing verb forms.

Present Tense	Past Tense
	flew
	paid
swim	
write	
	jumped
speak	
go	
	bought

Listening and Speaking

A. Listen to a bird talk about how she makes her nest. Now imagine that you are a rook. All your friends are impressed by your skill in building a nest and want to learn the secret. Tell them the process of building a nest using clear and simple instructions.

Pen it Down

Write a poem about the plants and animals you see around you.

You can use the following points:

- how you feel when you see, smell or touch something related to Nature
- a happy memory related to Nature

Use the following rhyming words in your poem:

light–night sky–why tree–free flower–shower blue–true

4

Holiday Activities

Comprehension

Read the passage and answer the questions.

A new green pit viper species, which is a snake variety, was discovered in a natural environment in the Himalayan region. It has been named Salazar's pit viper, after Salazar Slytherin, a character from J.K. Rowling's much-loved *Harry Potter* series about magic.

The lead researcher, Zeeshan A. Mirza, and two other authors on the paper are big fans of the *Harry Potter* series. Mirza said, 'This was a tribute to the most fascinating story I have ever read during my childhood.'

In the *Harry Potter* novels, Salazar Slytherin is described as a Parselmouth, or one who can speak the language of snakes.

Salazar's pit viper is nocturnal and so is mainly active at night. There is a unique reddish-to-orange stripe present on the head and body of males. This variety of snake was discovered during an expedition to Northeast India during the summer of 2019.

The first snake was spotted resting on some creepers along a road. Mirza said, 'A glimpse of the species was enough to let us all know that it was something interesting and something that we had not seen before. The snake had a well-defined rusty red stripe along the face and the entire body unlike any species from Northeast India to our knowledge.'

Pit vipers are named after their heat-sensing pit organ, located between the nostril and the eye on both sides of the head. The pit organ is what allows them to sense the heat given off by their prey in the dark.

Salazar's pit viper was found in the state of Arunachal Pradesh, which is where many new discoveries of plants and animals have been made in recent decades.

A. Tick [✓] the correct options.

1. The new species of pit viper was found in

   (a) Himachal Pradesh. (b) Arunachal Pradesh. (c) Madhya Pradesh.

2. The pit viper is named after a series of books by

   (a) J. K. Rowling. (b) Enid Blyton. (c) Ruskin Bond.

3. The lead researcher's name is

(a) Zeeshan A. Mirza. (b) Harry Potter. (c) Salazar Slytherin.

4. Salazar Slytherin is a

(a) lead researcher. (b) pit viper. (c) character from *Harry Potter*.

B. Briefly answer the following questions.

1. What is the name of the new species of pit viper?

2. What does the word Parselmouth mean?

3. When and in which region of India was the pit viper discovered?

C. Read the line from the passage and answer the questions.

'A new green pit viper species, which is a snake variety, was discovered in a natural environment in the Himalayan region.'

a. Why was the new pit viper named Salazar's pit viper?

b. What are pit vipers named after?

c. Where is the pit organ located?

d. What is the function of the pit organ?

Way with Words

A. Complete the sentences with to, too or two.

1. Ranveer has ________ projects ________ submit tomorrow.
2. The ________ of us have ________ perform on stage.
3. You have ________ wait for ________ years before you can participate in the dance competition.
4. You are ________ young ________ to drive a car.
5. I would like ________ borrow your bicycle for ________ weeks.

Words Related to Travel

B. Match the words in column A with their meaning in column B.

Column A	Column B
1. sleeping bag	a. you put your things in this before you go on a holiday
2. suitcase	b. a device used to capture photographs for memory
3. tent	c. a basket used to carry food for a picnic
4. hamper	d. the covering you sleep in when you sleep outdoors
5. camera	e. a movable shelter made of cloth

C. Complete the sentences with suitable words from the box.

ticket   luggage   photographs   pleasant   train

1. I went to Agra by ______________ to see the Taj Mahal.
2. We had very little ______________ with us.
3. At the ______________ counter, I bought five entry tickets for my family.
4. At the Taj Mahal, we took some beautiful ______________.
5. The weather was ______________ all along, so we enjoyed the day a lot.

Grammar in Use

Prepositions of Time and Place

A **preposition** is a word that shows the relation between a noun or a pronoun and the other words in the sentence.

Prepositions of time are used to talk about a point of time or a period of time/duration.
Examples: Our mother does not let us go out **in** the afternoon. (*in* – point of time)
We've been here **for** almost two weeks. (*for* – period of time/duration)

Prepositions of place are used to talk about a point or a place that can be identified.
Examples: Vivaan went **to** Calcutta last week. (*to* – direction)
This fruit grows **on** very thorny trees, but it is very yummy. (*on* – position)

A. Complete these sentences with the correct prepositions from the brackets.

1. The plastic packet was kept ______________ the mattress. (on/in)
2. My father is going ______________ (to/by) Egypt ______________ work. (through/for)
3. We go to school ______________ bus. (by/to)
4. The naughty boy threw a stone ______________ the dog. (on/at)
5. My grandfather always wakes up early ______________ the morning. (by/in)

Comparison of Adjectives

You have learned that to compare a particular quality of two things or persons, we add **-er** to the adjective. When we compare something with more than two things or persons, we add **-est** to the adjective to show that it has the highest degree of that particular quality.

Example: bright—brighter—brightest

Some adjectives don't take on the **-er/-est** form. In such cases, we add **more** or **most** before the adjective.

Example: Priti's painting is beautiful. Sheela's painting is **more beautiful** than Priti's. Seema's painting is the **most beautiful**.

B. Complete the sentences with the suitable form of the adjectives given in brackets.

1. My room is the ______________________ room in the house. (clean)
2. This is the ______________________ puzzle that I have ever solved. (interesting)
3. Lions are ______________________ than elephants. (dangerous)
4. Your watch is ______________________ than my watch. (expensive)
5. My cousin is ______________________ than me. (short)
6. Rihan is the ______________________ boy in class. (clever)

Listening and Speaking

A. What kind of activities do you like to do during your holidays? Work in pairs and tell your partner three things that you like doing. Let your partner respond with three things he/she likes to do during holidays.

Words that end in **-ed** can be pronounced in three ways.

Examples: wanted—the last **ed** sound is /id/
played—the last **ed** sound is /d/
hoped—the last **ed** sound is /t/

B. Read aloud the words given in the box. Identify the last -ed sound and write it under the correct column in the table on the next page.

mended	laughed	counted	cleaned	jumped	begged
brushed	ended	rolled	visited	banged	reached

wanted /id/	played /d/	hoped /t/

Pen it Down

Complete the following passage by filling in the blanks according to the instruction given in the brackets.

My school is planning a trip ____________ (preposition of place) Gujarat ____________ (preposition of time) August. The state is ____________ (comparative adjective of **beautiful**) than what ____________ (personal pronoun) see in pictures. We will stay there ____________ (preposition of time) a week. We will stay in a resort ____________ (preposition of place) top of a hillock. Among all the students, my best friend is the ____________ (superlative adjective of **excited**) as her grandparents live in Gujarat. The trip is ____________ (preposition of time) the 2nd of August ____________ (preposition of time) the 8th of August. ____________ (personal pronoun) will really be an enjoyable experience for all of us.

5 The History of Chocolate

Way with Words

Homophones

A. Complete the sentences with the correct homophones.

1. I __________ that I am going to represent my school in the talent show. (know/no)
2. My aunt has been living in Australia for ten __________. (years/ears)
3. Rajan __________ the bed before he went out to play. (maid/made)
4. We should always wash __________ hands before we eat. (hour/our)
5. The children kept __________ belongings inside the lockers. (there/their)
6. Mr Basu had to __________ off his old computer. (sell/cell)

Contextual Usage

B. Read the clues and complete the crossword.

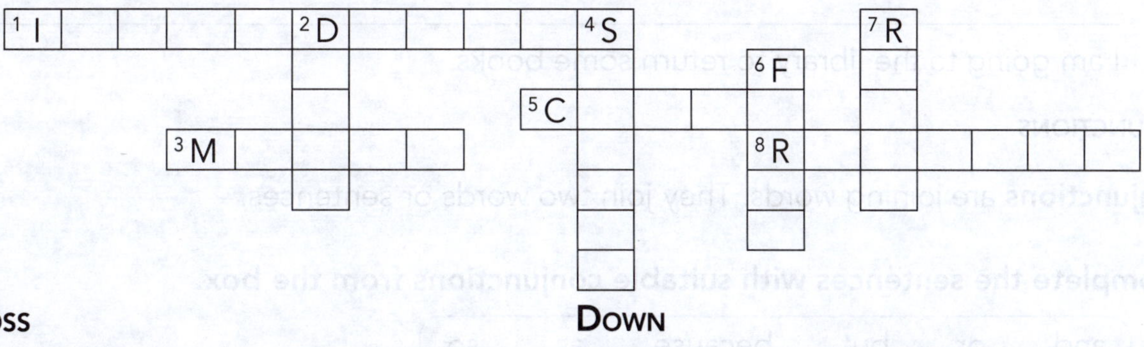

Across

1. the Aztec used cocoa beans as this
3. we use this to buy things like chocolate
5. food of the gods
8. in the factories, the beans are __________

Down

2. the first chocolate was not a bar but this
4. these explorers conquered Central America
6. each pod contains these many beans
7. members of these families served chocolate at their weddings

C. Complete these sentences with the words and phrases from the box.

look after	ingredients	harvest	bitter	mould

1. I __________ my sister when my mother is away.

2. Most children do not like ________________ medicines.
3. We require four ________________ to make this recipe.
4. Pour hot chocolate into the ________________ to set it.
5. We had a good ____________ of tomatoes this year as the weather was good.

Grammar in Use

QUESTION WORDS

We use words such as **what**, **where**, **who**, **why**, **when** and **how** to ask questions.

A. Frame questions for these answers.

1. Sarita is nine years old.
   ____
2. My favourite author is Roald Dahl.
   ____
3. My uncle gave me a watch on my birthday.
   ____
4. I could not come yesterday because I was not well.
   ____
5. The train will leave the station at nine o'clock.
   ____
6. I am going to the library to return some books.

CONJUNCTIONS

Conjunctions are joining words. They join two words or sentences.

B. Complete the sentences with suitable conjunctions from the box.

and	or	but	because	as	so

1. Do you want to watch television ________ read a book?
2. I like to eat apples ________ oranges.
3. I carried an umbrella ________ it was raining.
4. Zeena went off to sleep ________ she was very tired.
5. The water in the pool was nice and cold ________ we did not swim.
6. Naman is not well, ____ he will not come to play today.

Listening and Speaking

A. Listen to the words and write them down.

B. Work in pairs. Describe the process of making chocolate to your partner. Then, take turns to ask and answer questions.

Pen it Down

Look at the picture given below and write a paragraph about it. You can use the following points to help you:

- tourists in Paris
- food and drinks loved by the locals
- having food outdoors
- taste – sweet/bitter, hot/cold
- overall experience

6 The Elf and the Dormouse

Way with Words

A. Find the names of these fantasy characters in the word grid.

elf gnome fairy pixie dwarf goblin genie

G	N	O	M	E	A	B	C	D	E	F	G
H	I	J	K	L	M	N	O	P	Q	R	S
T	U	V	W	F	A	I	R	Y	X	Y	Z
A	B	C	D	E	F	H	G	I	J	K	L
M	N	O	P	Q	R	G	O	B	L	I	N
S	T	P	I	X	I	E	U	V	W	X	Y
Z	A	B	C	D	E	N	F	G	H	I	J
K	L	M	N	O	P	I	Q	R	S	T	U
D	W	A	R	F	V	E	W	X	Y	A	Z

Expressions

The exclamation mark (!) is generally used after words, phrases and sentences that express the emotions of joy, sorrow, a wish or a surprise.

Example: Congratulations! You have come first in your class.

B. Fill in with the correct word from the box to complete the expressions.

Wow Look Bravo Oh Hurrah

1. __________! My team has won the match.
2. __________! This painting is beautiful.
3. __________! The police caught the criminal.
4. __________! There is a shooting star in the sky.
5. __________! I failed to submit my homework on time.

Grammar in Use

Common and Proper Nouns

A **common noun** refers to people, places, animals or things in general.

Examples: elf, dormouse

A **proper noun** refers to a special name of a person, place, animal or thing that helps to identify it. Proper names begin with a capital letter.

Examples: **Oliver** writes beautiful poems.

A. Read the following passage and identify the common and proper nouns. Then, place the nouns in the correct column.

Sanvi and Sunaina are sisters. They go to school together every day. They usually take a bus, but if the weather is pleasant, they ride their bicycles. They often meet their teacher, Mrs Sen, after they cross the school gate. She teaches them English. They greet her with a smile and then go to the classroom. Their best friend in class is Priti and they always sit beside her.

Proper Noun	Common Noun

Inverted Commas

We use inverted commas to indicate the direct words of the speaker. Inverted commas are also used at the beginning and end of a quotation and to highlight a particular word in a sentence. Single inverted commas are used to show the title of a book, essay or a poem.

B. Rewrite the sentences using inverted commas in the correct places.

1. We are going to Nainital for a holiday, my father said.

   ____

2. The teacher said, I will attend the meeting on Friday.

   ____

3. What a wonderful painting! said the judge.

   ____

4. When will you return the book to the library, mother asked John.

____

5. Shakespeare's play The Merchant of Venice has been staged a number of times.

____

6. I was asked to recite The Elf and the Dormouse by Oliver Herford.

____

Listening and Speaking

Read the poem 'The Dog' by Oliver Herford with proper intonation. Write down all the rhyming words from the poem in the blanks given after the poem. One is done for you.

The Dog is black or white or brown
And sometimes spotted like a clown.
He loves to make a foolish noise
And Human Company enjoys.
The Human People pat his head
And teach him to pretend he's dead,
And beg, and fetch and carry too;
Things that no well-bred Cat will do.
At Human jokes, however stale,
He jumps about and wags his tail,
And Human People clap their hands
And think he really understands.
They say 'Good Dog' to him. To us
They say 'Poor Puss,' and make no fuss.
Why Dogs are 'good' and Cats are 'poor'
I fail to understand, I'm sure.
To Someone very Good and Just,
Who has proved worthy of her trust,
A Cat will sometimes condescend—
The Dog is Everybody's friend.

brown-clown _______________ _______________

_______________ _______________

_______________ _______________

_______________ _______________

Pen it Down

All of us look forward to the rainy season as it brings relief after the hot and humid summer. Write a paragraph describing the sights and sounds that we come across during the monsoons.

7

The Seed of Truth

Way with Words

Proverbs

A **proverb** is a short saying that shares wisdom related to common sense.

A. Match the proverbs in column A with their meanings in column B. One is done for you.

Column A	Column B
1. You can't judge a book by its cover.	a. What you do is more important than what you say.
2. Always put your best foot forward.	b. Cleanliness is a good virtue.
3. Actions speak louder than words.	c. It is good to be careful rather than regret our actions later.
4. As you sow, so shall you reap.	d. You should not judge someone based on their appearance.
5. Cleanliness is next to godliness.	e. Always do the best that you can.
6. It is better to be safe than sorry.	f. Your actions will decide what happens next.

B. Add ful or tion to these words and write the new words in the blanks. Make the necessary changes in spelling if required.

1. hope ____________
2. act ____________
3. wonder ____________
4. care ____________
5. harm ____________
6. success ____________
7. decorate ____________
8. educate ____________

Grammar in Use

Types of Sentences

A **statement** is a type of sentence that tells about an idea or says something.
A **question** is a type of sentence that asks something.
An **exclamation** is a type of sentence that shows a feeling.
A **command** is a type of sentence that is used to give orders.
A **request** is a type of sentence that is used to ask someone for something.

A. Identify these sentences. Write S for statement, Q for question, C for command and E for exclamation.

1. What a hot day it is! ____________
2. When will your summer holidays start? ____________
3. Shut the door and switch on the light. ____________
4. Children enjoy eating ice cream on a hot summer day. ____________
5. How will you reach the station on time? ____________
6. How beautifully Neerja sang! ____________

Definite and Indefinite Articles

A, *an* and *the* are called **articles**.
A and **an** are called indefinite articles as they do not refer to any particular person or object.
Example: My mother ate **an** egg. (any egg)
The is called definite article as it refers to a particular person or object.
Example: My mother ate **the** egg that I had boiled. (a particular egg)

B. Insert articles wherever required and rewrite the sentences.

1. Taj Mahal is famous tourist spot.
____
2. King lives in palace in Nepal.
____

3. Reena bought expensive necklace from shop.
____
4. My aunt lives in huge house in middle of town.
____
5. Highest mountain in world is Mount Everest.
____
6. My father has to attend meeting tomorrow.
____

Listening and Speaking

A. Listen to the passage and write whether the sentences are true (T) or false (F).

1. As a child, Midas used to watch the ants running around. ☐
2. Ants used to carry gold pieces from one place to the other. ☐
3. Midas decided he will never work as hard as the ants. ☐
4. Adding more treasure to his treasury made him sad. ☐
5. He increased the taxes on his subjects for his greed. ☐
6. The most precious thing to him was the gold. ☐

B. Do you know any story about honesty and truthfulness? Work in groups of four and narrate the story to your friends.

Write the name of the story here:

____

Pen it Down

Write a paragraph explaining the proverb 'Honesty is the best policy'. You can use the following points in your paragraph:

- explain the words in the proverb
- describe any incident/event where being honest led to a positive result
- share what you learnt from that experience
- mention if you believe in the proverb, and why

____

____

____

____

____

____

____

____

____

8

Breakfast

Way with Words

Compound Words Related to Food

A. Match the words given in the two columns to form food items. Then, make sentences with any four compound words.

A	B
1. ice	a. sauce
2. french	b. cake
3. mango	c. lollies
4. butter	d. rings
5. cheese	e. fries
6. onion	f. bread
7. apple	g. shake
8. ginger	h. milk

Words Related to Smell

B. Fill in the blanks with words related to smell from the box.

rotten fruity fresh smoky earthy

1. Did you use peach shampoo? Your hair smells __________.
2. The lawn looks so clean and has an __________ smell after the rains.
3. My uncle makes the most delicious roast potatoes with a __________ aroma.
4. I like the __________ fragrance of jasmine flowers coming from the garden.
5. Throw away the stale fish from the fridge. They smell __________.

Grammar in Use

Agreement of Subject and Verb

The verb in a sentence must agree with the subject of the sentence. If the subject is singular, then the verb must be singular; and if the subject is plural, then the verb must be plural.

A. Complete the sentences using the present tense form of suitable verbs.

1. The children ____________ their homework regularly.
2. Aman ____________ in a huge bungalow.
3. Priya always ____________ her teachers in the morning.
4. My jeans ____________ torn, so I will buy a new pair.
5. The exercise books ____________ on the teacher's desk.
6. I ____________ a glass of milk every day.

Conditional Sentences

In a sentence, we use **if** to show that the main action can only take place if a condition is fulfilled.

B. Combine the two sentences using if.

1. I am rich. I must buy a car.

   ____

2. I will go out to play. I must complete my revision.

   ____

3. Fiza has ₹500. She will buy a new watch.

   ____

4. You must come first in class. You will get a new study table.

   ____

5. I will go for a morning walk. I must wake up early.

   ____

6. You can have an ice cream. You must eat lunch.

   ____

7. You are weak. You must take care of your diet.

   ____

8. You can play with your friends. You must eat your dinner.

   ____

Listening and Speaking

Have a class discussion with your teacher about buying local and seasonal food. Then, state whether the following statements are true or false.

1. Grocery stores offer local food at a lower price. ☐
2. Seasonal and local food have more health benefits. ☐
3. When we buy local food, we can reduce the risk of food wastage. ☐
4. The money we spend to buy local and seasonal food doesn't help farmers. ☐
5. Canned food is healthier than fresh food. ☐

Pen it Down

Make a list of healthy food habits. Then make a table with two columns. Write the advantages of eating healthy food in column A and the disadvantages of having junk food in column B.

Healthy Food Habits

Column A	Column B

9 Adventure at the Circus

Way with Words

Sometimes, different words have similar meanings.
Example: Both the words **gobble** and **nibble** mean 'to eat' something.

A. Complete the sentences with suitable words from the box.

bite	nibble	chew	gobble	feed

1. Raj took a __________ of his burger and then had a sip of water.
2. We must __________ our food properly.
3. Gargi tried to __________ up her breakfast as she was getting late for school.
4. The kind king used to __________ all the beggars outside the temple.
5. The squirrel likes to __________ at the nuts.

Movement Verbs

B. Given below are some movement words. Complete the sentences using their past tense form.

march	leap	drag	crawl	dive
chase	run	glide	gallop	fly

1. The baby __________ across the carpet.
2. Did you see how smartly the soldiers __________ in the parade?
3. The boy __________ over the hurdle and won the race.
4. Rohini __________ the bag as it was very heavy.
5. The instructor __________ into the swimming pool from great height.
6. The boy __________ the butterflies in the garden.
7. The birds __________ away when I opened the cage.
8. My horse __________ gracefully at the parade.
9. The kite __________ in the sky for a while before it fell on the ground.
10. Mohan __________ away when he saw the scary shadow on the wall.

Grammar in Use

ADVERBS

An **Adverb** is a word that adds meaning to a verb. It tells us something more about the action in a sentence.

Example: He stood **quietly** in a corner.

A. Write a suitable adverb for each verb. Then make sentences with the verb-adverb pairs.

1. walk ________________
2. write ________________
3. read ________________
4. enter ________________
5. dance ________________
6. drive ________________
7. speak ________________
8. watch ________________

____

____

____

____

____

____

____

____

____

____

____

____

B. Fill in the blanks with the adverbs given in the box.

swiftly	peacefully	nearly	wisely	certainly	slowly

1. The old man spoke ___________.
2. My grandmother walked ___________ on the uneven path.
3. The baby was sleeping ___________.
4. The athlete ran ___________ in order to win the race.
5. I have ___________ completed my project.
6. My parents will ___________ attend the meeting

Listening and Speaking

A. Listen carefully to words that make the /s/ sound and the /sh/ sound and say them aloud.

B. Work in pairs. Take turns to ask and give permission to do the following:

a. Go out and play.
b. Use the computer.
c. Open the window.
d. Borrow the book from Ram.
e. Sit down.

Pen it Down

Make a poster about an adventure trip. You must include the following details:

- the location or the place
- various activities that can be done there
- the duration of stay and the cost
- one unique feature of the trip

Draw or paste some pictures to make the poster look more appealing.

Test Paper

Comprehension

A. Read this poem by Charles Lamb carefully and answer the questions.

The First Tooth

Through the house what busy joy,
Just because the infant boy
Has a tiny tooth to show!
I have got a double row,
All as white, and all as small;
Yet no one cares for mine at all.
He can say but half a word,
Yet that single sound's preferred
To all the words that I can say
In the longest summer day.
He cannot walk, yet if he put
With mimic motion out his foot,
As if he thought he were advancing,
It's prized more than my best dancing.

1. Why was everyone at home very happy?

   ____

2. Do you think the poet was jealous of his baby brother? Give reasons for your answer.

   ____

3. How did the baby pretend that he could walk?

   ____

4. Complete the following sentences.

   a. The infant boy has a ______________________________.

   b. The baby's false steps are prized more ______________________________.

   c. The poet has a double row of teeth, all ______________________________.

Way with Words

A. Complete the sentences with words/phrases from the box.

adventure	hunting	rafting
bathe in the stream	picnic	picking fruit

1. The king went on a ____________________ trip with his ministers.
2. All the children were happily ____________________ in the orchard.
3. I love to read ____________________ stories.
4. Rahul loves to ____________________ when he visits his grandparents in the village.
5. One of the adventure sports during the summer camp was __________.
6. The teacher took all the students for a ____________________ to Eco Park.

B. Read the clues and write the word. All the words are from the stories and begin with the letter 'm'.

1. babies drink this: ____________________
2. tiny flowerless plants that grow on damp ground: ____________________
3. hollow containers used to give shape to hot liquids when they cool and harden: ____________________
4. a unit of measurement: ____________________
5. 12 of them in a year: ____________________
6. present tense of *made*: ____________________

C. Change one letter at a time to form new words.

BEND	CASH
↓	↓
__ __ __ __	__ __ __ __
↓	↓
__ __ __ __	__ __ __ __
↓	↓
SEEP	MUST

D. Circle the odd one in each set.

1. elf, gnome, pixie, rabbit
2. rafting, shooting, reading, hunting
3. dolphin, turtle, elephant, fish

4. milk, juice, water, fruits
5. kingfisher, salmon, woodpecker, toucan
6. tooth, tongue, book, nail
7. dancing, playing, boxing, table
8. house, flat, apartment, village
9. summer, day, winter, monsoon
10. chair, table, stove, bed

E. Rearrange the letters to form words. All the words are from the stories.

1. dlicoeisu ____________ 5. oorcedk ____________
2. epxinecere ____________ 6. mrteeantt ____________
3. maetsr ____________ 7. tedimerne ____________
4. grintiende ____________ 8. stodaloot ____________

F. Write the opposite gender for the given words.

1. count ____________ 4. duke ____________
2. nephew ____________ 5. monk ____________
3. wizard ____________ 6. son ____________

Grammar in Use

A. Write three adjectives for each noun.

1. village ________, ________, ________
2. umbrella ________, ________, ________
3. elf ________, ________, ________
4. grandmother ________, ________, ________
5. teacher ________, ________, ________
6. mouse ________, ________, ________

B. Complete the sentences with suitable proper and common nouns.

1. My best friend ____________ is good at ____________.
2. My ____________ lives in the city of ____________.
3. The ____________ that I am reading is titled ____________.
4. During my ____________ holidays, I am going to ____________.
5. My cousin ____________ is in the school ____________ team.
6. Parth's elder sister ____________ is a ____________ by profession.

C. Complete the table with the correct form of the verbs.

Past	Present	Future
	hop	
		will sweep
	write	
brought		
		will speak
	go	

D. Underline the correct prepositions to complete the sentences.

1. Geeta leaned her bicycle (against/beside) the newly painted fence.
2. My sister was born (on/in) the month of July.
3. On her birthday, Roshni distributed sweets (among/between) her friends.
4. (Beside/Besides) a laptop, my cousin has a notepad and a desktop.
5. Rajan dived (inside/into) the swimming pool.
6. The naughty boy was hiding (near/behind) the door.

E. Complete the paragraph with suitable pronouns.

Raj and his brother visited the Indian museum last Sunday. The museum was very big. ________ was very crowded. ________ met their school friends there. ________ were very happy to see ________. All of ________ decided to explore the place together. First, ________ went to the Egyptian gallery. ________ had many artefacts, statutes and a model mummy. Then ________ visited the textile room. ________ were amazed by the variety of material that is produced all over the country.

Listening and Speaking

Have you ever visited a dentist? Share your experience with your class.

Pen it Down

During a football match, a member of the opponent team slipped and fell, injuring his/her leg badly. Write two paragraphs based on this situation. Do not exceed 100 words.

You can use the following points to write the paragraph:

- why the player slipped and fell

- what you did at that moment
- how the coach/referee reacted
- how the other students reacted
- what happened finally

10

Two Little Kittens

Way with Words

Rhyming Words

A. Write two rhyming words for each of the following:

1. free: ______________, ______________
2. night: ______________, ______________
3. dawn: ______________, ______________
4. late: ______________, ______________
5. cake: ______________, ______________
6. fear: ______________, ______________

Prefixes

B. Add the prefixes un-, dis-, in- or im- to the following words and write the new words.

1. comfort ________	4. believable ________	7. cover ________
2. correct ________	5. visible ________	8. honour ________
3. perfect ________	6. respect ________	9. proper ________

Grammar in Use

Contractions

Contractions are used to shorten a particular word. The missing letters are replaced with the apostrophe.

A. Rewrite the sentences using contractions, wherever necessary.

1. Jenny cannot read fluently.

____

2. I will go with you to the market.

3. We will collect food items for the Nepal earthquake victims.

4. I am going to Sri Lanka for a holiday.

5. Who is knocking at the door?

6. You have two weeks to complete the project.

Negative Sentences with *Not*

B. Rewrite the following sentences as negative sentences with 'not'. One has been done for you.

Example: We love to play football.
We do not love to play football.

1. I like to read a book every day.

2. He rides his bicycle every Sunday.

3. They switch off the lights before leaving the room.

4. Renu cleans her bedroom regularly.

5. My father was late for the meeting.

6. Sabrina has a pet dog.

Listening and Speaking

Your siblings are having an argument about which breed of dog they would like to keep as a pet. As the older sibling, you volunteer to help them solve the disagreement in a friendly manner. In groups of three, do a role play of the conversation.

You can use these phrases in the conversation:

- Please speak, one by one.
- What is the issue?
- Indian or a breed such as the Labrador?
- Let's listen to both sides.

Pen it Down

Your friend lent you her storybook for the weekend. While reading it, you accidentally spilled juice on it. Write a letter of apology to your friend and tell her that you will buy her a new book to replace the one that you damaged.

Women in Science

11

Anna's Experiments with Weather

Way with Words

Homophones

A **homophone** is a word that is pronounced the same as another word but has a different meaning.

A. Choose the correct word to complete the sentences.

1. The car skidded as the driver was not able to apply the ________. (brake/break)
2. My family and friends are very ____________ to me. (deer/dear)
3. My grandmother narrated the ___________ of the cunning fox. (tale/tail)
4. What is the ____________ of that red watch? (prize/price)
5. The children ate _________ many sweets at the birthday party. (too/two)
6. Ravi slept the __________ morning as he was quite unwell. (whole/hole)
7. I have not ___________ the newspaper today. (red/read)
8. The traveller ________ on a path that was covered with loose stones. (road/rode)

B. Complete the sentences with the correct homophones.

1. I don't know __________ we have a computer class today. (weather/whether)
2. His __________ were smelling because he had not washed them properly. (feet/feat)
3. The painting was __________ beautiful. (quiet/quite)
4. The car has been waiting __________ for the past one hour. (here/hear)
5. He wrote his address on a __________ of paper. (piece/peace)
6. It will take a long time for the wound to __________. (heel/heal)

Grammar in Use

Subject and Predicate

The **subject** denotes **whom** or what we are talking about. When we say something about the subject, it is called the **predicate**. A predicate always includes a verb.

A. Underline the subject and circle the predicate in the following sentences.

1. I will submit my project tomorrow.
2. My maternal aunt is an interior designer.
3. The heavy box was lifted by my friend.
4. Robin's grandfather is the coach of the school football team.
5. The gardener waters the plants regularly.
6. The thief managed to escape from the police station.

Possessive and Demonstrative Pronouns

Possessive pronouns are used to show ownership.

Example: These books are **mine**.

Demonstrative pronouns are used to point to something.

Example: **This** is my book.

B. Fill in with appropriate possessive and demonstrative pronouns.

1. Mohit has a red bag. The bag on the table is ______________.
2. They have a car. That car is ______________.
3. You have a plastic toy. The toy is ______________.
4. ______________ was such an interesting play.
5. We have a beautiful house. That house is ______________.
6. Are ______________ your books?

Listening and Speaking

Listen carefully to the announcement of a weather forecast by the India Meteorological Department and answer the following questions.

1. Which two states will get very heavy rainfall?

____

2. When will it start raining more heavily?

3. Which areas will experience very strong winds?

4. Why is there a red alert?

5. What may get damaged due to rough weather?

Pen it Down

Imagine that the weather department has forecasted a cyclone in your city in the next two days. You and your family have decided to leave your home for a safer location. Make a list of the items that you would need during your stay away from home.

You may use the following ideas to make your list:

- food
- clothing
- medicines
- ways to spend free time

12

Kangaroos

Way with Words

Words with Multiple Meanings

We often come across words that have two or more different meanings.

Example: watch– 1. to see
2. a device we wear on the wrist to tell time

A. Make two sentences with each word to bring out the difference in their meanings.

1. box ____________________
____
2. head ____________________
____
3. plain ____________________
____

B. Complete the sentences with the correct word from the box. You may have to change the form of the word where necessary.

flow	dodge	jump	bounce	hit	roll	creep	march

1. The stream ____________ into the main river.
2. The lady was ____________ on the ground in pain.
3. It is the duty of soldiers to learn to ____________ well.

4. I had to ____________ the ball to avoid getting hit on the head.
5. Pratik ____________ over the hurdles and won the race.
6. The thief ____________ into the house when everyone was asleep.
7. The ball ____________ three times before it stopped.
8. Let us ____________ the ball with the new bat.

Grammar in Use

Verb and Object

A. Read the sentences carefully. Identify and write the verb and the object, if any, in the blanks.

	V	O
1. Ravi was playing with the ball.	________	________
2. The dog was barking.	________	________
3. We read an interesting book.	________	________
4. Manish leaned against the pole.	________	________
5. The choir sang melodiously.	________	________
6. The carpenter made a beautiful bed.	________	________
7. We painted the wall blue.	________	________
8. Mala drank the juice quickly.	________	________
9. Vicky bought a big teddy bear.	________	________
10. Siya laughed loudly.	________	________

Negative Contractions

Some verbs that are followed by **not** can be shortened by replacing -**o**- with an apostrophe.

Examples: **was not → wasn't**
could not → couldn't

B. Answer the questions using can't, couldn't, won't or wouldn't.

1. Can you go out to play now?
   No, ______________________________.
2. Will you lend me your PSP?
   No, ______________________________.
3. Would you like to have paneer pizza?
   No, ______________________________.
4. Can you buy me a notebook?
   No, ______________________________.
5. Would you like to participate in the dance competition?
   No, ______________________________.
6. Can you wake up early tomorrow?
   No, ______________________________.

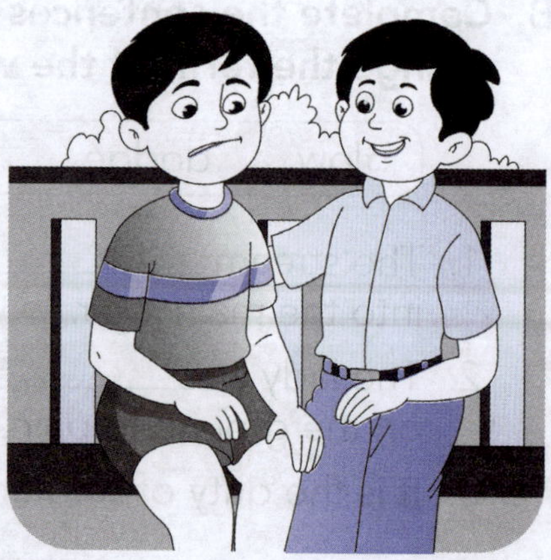

12 Kangaroos

Way with Words

Words with Multiple Meanings

We often come across words that have two or more different meanings.

Example: watch– 1. to see
2. a device we wear on the wrist to tell time

A. Make two sentences with each word to bring out the difference in their meanings.

1. box ______________________________
____
2. head ______________________________
____
3. plain ______________________________
____

B. Complete the sentences with the correct word from the box. You may have to change the form of the word where necessary.

flow	dodge	jump	bounce	hit	roll	creep	march

1. The stream ______________ into the main river.
2. The lady was ______________ on the ground in pain.
3. It is the duty of soldiers to learn to ______________ well.
4. I had to ______________ the ball to avoid getting hit on the head.
5. Pratik ______________ over the hurdles and won the race.
6. The thief ______________ into the house when everyone was asleep.
7. The ball ______________ three times before it stopped.
8. Let us ______________ the ball with the new bat.

Grammar in Use

Verb and Object

A. Read the sentences carefully. Identify and write the verb and the object, if any, in the blanks.

	V	O
1. Ravi was playing with the ball.	______	______
2. The dog was barking.	______	______
3. We read an interesting book.	______	______
4. Manish leaned against the pole.	______	______
5. The choir sang melodiously.	______	______
6. The carpenter made a beautiful bed.	______	______
7. We painted the wall blue.	______	______
8. Mala drank the juice quickly.	______	______
9. Vicky bought a big teddy bear.	______	______
10. Siya laughed loudly.	______	______

Negative Contractions

Some verbs that are followed by **not** can be shortened by replacing **-o-** with an apostrophe.

Examples: **was not → wasn't**
could not → couldn't

B. Answer the questions using can't, couldn't, won't or wouldn't.

1. Can you go out to play now?
   No, ________________________.
2. Will you lend me your PSP?
   No, ________________________.
3. Would you like to have paneer pizza?
   No, ________________________.
4. Can you buy me a notebook?
   No, ________________________.
5. Would you like to participate in the dance competition?
   No, ________________________.
6. Can you wake up early tomorrow?
   No, ________________________.

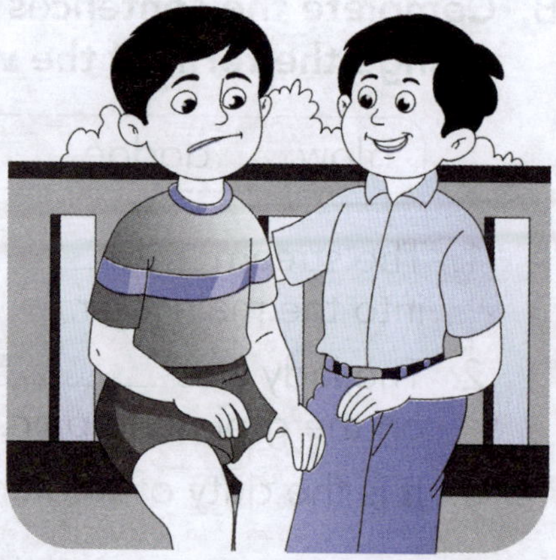

Listening and Speaking

Read the words aloud and write them in the correct column according to the sound of i in them.

grin time bike fish wig dice hit size

Short i as in *king*	Long i as in *smile*

Pen it Down

You know that the kangaroo is the national animal of Australia. Write five lines each on the national bird and national animal of India. Draw their pictures too.

13 Amparo's Journey

Comprehension

Read the passage and answer the questions.

This story took place in Africa. One day, Baboon decided to leave the tree where he lived and made a new home next to the river. He told all the other animals that the land belonged to him so only he could drink from the river.

The animals were sad because they needed water to survive. But all of them were afraid of Baboon. He had a big head with thick eyebrows and sharp teeth.

Zebra was young, brave and handsome in his pure white coat. Zebra said to the animals, 'I am not afraid of Baboon. I will tell him we are going to drink from the river.'

The next day, Zebra met with Baboon. He challenged Baboon to a fight. It had been a long time since Baboon had lost a fight. They agreed that the loser would leave the jungle and the river. They decided to meet the next morning.

The following day, Zebra came to Baboon's yard. Baboon had built a bonfire. All the animals came to watch the fight. Baboon and Zebra were both strong and used all their skills. Zebra used his powerful legs to run at Baboon. But Baboon was very swift and quickly jumped out of Zebra's way.

Before Zebra could stop, he was suddenly close to the bonfire. The heat from the fire began to burn him. Zebra turned around and kicked Baboon, making him fall hard on the ground. Baboon wasn't injured, but he accepted that he had lost.

Zebra won, but the fire had left long black stripes on his white coat. From then, all zebras had black stripes and were proud of them. These were a symbol of Zebra's victory over Baboon so that all animals could drink water from the river.

A. Fill in the blanks with suitable words from the passage.

1. This story took place in __________.
2. In the beginning, Baboon used to live on a __________.
3. All the animals were afraid of __________.
4. Baboon had built a __________ in his yard.
5. Zebra used his powerful __________ to run at Baboon.

B. Arrange the sentences in the order of events in the passage.

1. All the animals came to watch the fight.
2. Zebra kicked Baboon over the river.
3. Baboon decided to live near the river.
4. Zebra challenged Baboon to a fight.
5. Baboon did not allow the other animals to drink from the river.

C. Read the line from the passage and answer the questions.

'I will tell him we are going to drink from the river.'

1. Who said these words and to whom?

   ____

2. Who does 'him' refer to?

   ____

3. What happened when Zebra got close to the fire?

   ____

   ____

4. Why are zebras proud of their black stripes?

   ____

   ____

Way with Words

A. Circle all the words/phrases that mean the same as scared or suggest that someone is scared. Some of them are from the story.

1. gulped 2. shakily 3. sadly 4. went white 5. trembled
6. grumpy 7. gasped 8. fearful 9. afraid 10. uncomfortable

SUFFIXES

A **suffix** is a letter or group of letters placed at the end of a word to make a new word.

B. Complete the following sentences by adding a suffix to the words given in the box.

comfort	help	danger	child	use	exhibit	sad	cloud

1. It is __________ to play with fire.
2. I had a very enjoyable __________.
3. It was a __________ day.
4. My heart was filled with __________ when my best friend left the city.
5. These shoes are very __________.
6. The __________ boy picked up all the apples that had fallen from the basket.
7. My mother bought a beautiful dress for me at the __________.
8. Umbrellas are very __________ on rainy days.

Grammar in Use

Prepositional Phrases

A **prepositional phrase** is a group of words that starts with a preposition and ends with a noun or pronoun. It is used to tell more about a person or an action.

A. Complete the sentences with the correct options.

1. The house ______________ belongs to my uncle. (beside the lake/in the lake)
2. The crow laid the eggs ______________. (on the nest/in the nest)
3. The shop ______________ sells tasty momos. (behind the park/on the park)
4. The wooden bridge ______________ is not very strong. (beside the stream/over the stream)
5. I will take a short nap ______________. (at lunch/after lunch)
6. There is a beautiful vase ______________. (on the table/inside the table)

Present Continuous Tense

To form the present continuous tense, we use the helping verbs **is**, **am** or **are** with the *–ing* form of verbs.

Example: We **are playing** in the park.

B. Complete the sentences with the present continuous form of the verbs given in the brackets.

1. Rohan ______________ between Ravi and Farman. (sit)
2. My parents ______________ in a hotel in London. (stay)
3. We ______________ for a party tonight. (go)
4. The teacher ______________ a science magazine. (read)
5. My uncle ______________ all the dirty clothes. (wash)
6. The gardener ______________ a few trees. (plant)

C. Complete the sentences with the simple present and present continuous form of the verbs.

1. Riya ______________ to school by bus, but today she ______________ by car. (go)
2. Dhavan ______________ football today. These days he ______________ cricket regularly. (play)
3. Mother usually ______________ a book when she goes to sleep, but today she is very tired. (read)
4. Every morning she ______________ coffee but today she ______________ tea. (drink)
5. She ______________ in her room now. (sleep)
6. The dog ______________ after every passing car. (run)
7. It ______________ since last night. We could not go out to play. (rain)

Listening and Speaking

Along with your classmates, spin a story yarn. Each child has to contribute one sentence to carry the story forward. You must listen carefully to the previous speaker and then continue. Remember that the line you add to the story must answer the questions – where, which, when and how. The first line of the story is:

I reached school and realised that all my project material was at home...

Pen it Down

Look at the pictures carefully and write a story. You may use the following hints to write the story:

- a young lad
- suddenly found a treasure map
- did not disclose it to anyone
- went on the trip alone

Space Stories

14
The Land of Fib

Way with Words

Contextual Usage

A. Rearrange the letters to make meaningful words. All the words are from the chapter.

1. ocalcohet ______________
2. ethmnawrea ______________
3. pesrindet ______________
4. storaunat ______________
5. burllmea ______________
6. pranceapea ______________

Professions

You read about people who practise different professions, such as a news reporter, weatherman and doctor, in the chapter.

B. Find and circle eight professions in the grid given below.

V	W	X	Y	Z	A	W	A	I	T	E	R	C	D	B
P	I	J	K	L	M	N	O	P	Q	R	S	T	U	O
I	W	D	X	Y	Z	A	B	C	D	E	F	G	H	X
L	M	E	N	L	A	R	T	I	S	T	T	U	V	E
O	A	N	B	C	D	O	E	F	G	H	I	J	K	R
T	P	T	Q	R	S	L	T	U	V	W	X	Y	E	Z
D	E	I	F	G	T	E	A	C	H	E	R	G	N	O
N	T	S	U	V	W	I	S	X	Y	Z	N	A	B	C
F	G	T	H	I	J	E	K	L	M	I	O	P	Q	R
W	X	Y	Z	A	P	R	I	E	S	T	B	C	D	E
H	I	J	K	L	M	N	O	P	Q	R	S	T	U	V
R	E	P	O	R	T	E	R	G	F	E	D	C	B	A

Grammar in Use

Past Continuous Tense

The past continuous tense is used to describe an action that was going on in the past.
Example: The weatherman **was telling** lies to the audience.

A. Complete the sentences in the past continuous tense using the verbs given in the brackets.

1. Rahul ____________________ the dishes while father ____________________ dinner. (wash, cook)
2. The baby ____________________ because he was hungry. (cry)
3. The rabbit ____________________ the mouse. (chase)
4. While they ____________________ dinner, the doorbell rang. (have)

5. The dog ____________________ at the stranger. (bark)
6. The students ____________________ a concert. (watch)

The Comma

You know that commas are used to separate items in a list or to make a sentence easy to understand.
Example: The weatherman, the president, the doctor and the news reporters were all lying.

B. Rewrite the sentences by inserting commas and adding and wherever necessary.

1. Guests were served cookies cakes sweets some tea.
   ____
2. I bought a book few pencils a new table lamp for myself.
   ____
3. In flowers, she loves roses tulips orchids jasmine the most.
   ____
4. Ritika Deepika are the tallest girls in the class.
   ____
5. We visited the science museum art museum and in the end went to an amusement park.
   ____
6. Red blue green purple yellow coloured kites were flying in the sky.
   ____
7. I like reading short stories Pooja enjoys poems Rita likes to solve puzzles in her free time.
   ____

Listening and Speaking

Listen to the story and answer the questions orally.

1. What did the Little Alien decide?
2. What was the colour of the planet?
3. What did the Little Alien see on the planet?
4. Can you guess the name of the blue planet?

Pen it Down

In the story we learned that John, the astronaut, made the people of Fib realise the importance of truth. On behalf of the people of the Land of Fib, write a letter to thank John.

15 The Land of Counterpane

Way with Words

Contextual Usage

A. Complete the sentences with the words and phrases from the box.

soldiers	pillows	up and down
ships in fleets	for an hour	uniform

1. My __________________ became dirty because I played football in the rain.
2. The General inspired his __________________ to fight fearlessly.
3. The children were so happy that they started jumping __________________.
4. My mother had to go to office __________________.
5. We played passing the __________________ last evening.
6. The Indian Navy sent out the __________________ and the sight was majestic.

Odd One Out

B. Circle the odd one in each set.

1. sick	ill	unwell	disease
2. pillow	bedcover	curtain	mattress
3. sand	hill	plain	dale
4. city	town	country	atlas
5. sea	ships	boats	canoe
6. touch	head	chest	hand

Grammar in Use

Helping Verbs

A. Complete the sentences with suitable helping verbs.

1. The minister ____________ unfurling the Indian flag.
2. We ____________ reading a story from the *Panchatantra* in class.
3. Virat Kohli ____________ playing very well today.
4. The teachers ____________ having a meeting in the staffroom.
5. I ____________ doing an experiment in the science laboratory.
6. The school ____________ declaring a holiday on 1 May.
7. We ____________ cleaning the cupboard.

Modal Verbs

Modal verbs are helping verbs that indicate the mood or the tense of the action.
Can and **could** are used to show that something is possible, express an ability and ask for permission.
May is used to take formal permission and show possibility.
Must is used to talk about necessity and duty and to give command.
Will is used to talk about a future action and to give a solution to a problem.
Should is used to express duty, give advice and talk about something that is likely to happen.

B. Complete the sentences with suitable modals:

1. My mother __________ speak Japanese fluently.
2. Children __________ wear a uniform to school.
3. I __________ not remember his name though I met him last week.
4. We __________ not walk bare feet.
5. My friends __________ not reach the picnic spot on time.
6. My elder brother __________ drive a car.
7. Children __________ not play with sharp objects.
8. I __________ do better in my next assessment.
9. We __________ always obey our elders.
10. You __________ borrow my bicycle for a day.

Types of Adjectives

You have learned about about three different types of adjectives.

Adjectives of quality describe a quality of someone or something.

Example: The **sick** boy didn't go to school.

Adjectives of quantity tell us how many people, animals or things there are.

Example: The boy played with **many** toy ships.

Demonstrative adjectives point out particular people, animals or things.

Example: **That** pillow looks comfortable.

C. Fill in the blanks with suitable adjectives given in the box. Then, write down their type.

curly	friendly	seven
many	tall	that

1. Surbhi has ____________ hair.
2. ____________ book on the shelf is mine.
3. There are too ____________ mistakes in this essay.
4. Karan's dog is very ____________ .
5. There are ____________ days in a week.
6. There is a ____________ tree near my school.

Listening and Speaking

Words with *ea* can be pronounced with a long 'e' sound as in *seat* or a short 'e' sound as in *bread*.

Read the words aloud and write them in the correct column.

meat head deaf bead thread heal dead peach spread beak

Long e sound as in *seat*	Short e sound as in *bread*

Pen it Down

In the poem, the little boy plays with several toys, such as lead soldiers and ships. Make a list of five of your favourite toys and give a reason why you like playing with each of them.

16
Emily's Brush with History

Comprehension

Read the passage and answer the questions.

The structure of Egyptian society was like a pyramid. At the top were the gods — Ra, Osiris, Isis, and many others. Ancient Egyptians believed that the gods were very powerful, and they had to be kept happy. If the gods were angry, the rivers flooded, famines happened, and earthquakes shook the Earth.

The ancient Egyptians also gave the status of gods to some humans. Pharaohs were believed to be gods on Earth. They were buried in beautiful tombs inside stone pyramids after they died. This was done as a form of worship. The pharaohs were the religious, political and military leaders of the Egyptians. They were paid taxes in the form of grain which was stored in very big halls. This was used to feed the people during famines.

The chief minister appointed by the pharaoh was responsible for collecting taxes from people. All court activities were noted down by official record keepers. They were given a special place in society because they were educated while most people could not read or write. The priests who were between the pharaoh and the chief minister had the job of pleasing the gods. Below them were the wealthy nobles who held high government posts.

Next came the soldiers who fought for the pharaohs. They managed the slaves when there was no war. Doctors, traders, craftsmen and farmers made up the rest of Egyptian society.

Even if the working class could not become nobles or priests, they could educate their sons in schools run by the nobles. Women were not allowed to go to schools.

The slaves were at the bottom of Egyptian society. They were brought from different countries as prisoners of war. They had no rights and were treated like cattle.

A. Answer in a word or two.

1. they were at the top of Egyptian society: ____________
2. an Egyptian god: ____________
3. this happened if the gods were angry: ____________
4. they were at the bottom of society: ____________
5. they were not allowed to go to schools: ____________

B. Complete the following statements with information from the passage.

1. Ancient Egyptians believed that the gods ____________________.
2. The pharaohs were believed to be ________________.
3. The pharaohs were paid taxes in the form of ______________.
4. The priests were between the ____________ and ____________.
5. The slaves were treated ________________________.

C. Answer the following questions.

1. Where were the pharaohs buried?
____
____
2. What was the chief minister responsible for?
____
____
3. Why were the official record keepers given a special place in society?
____
____
4. What did the soldiers do?
____
____
5. Where were the slaves brought from?
____
____

Way with Words

COLLOCATIONS

A **collocation** is a combination of two words that are generally used together.
Examples: great crash, train station, capital city

A. Complete the following collocations using the words given in the box.

prepared	time	sleep	meeting	surprise
mistake	believe	tide	madness	rain

1. saving ______________
2. heavy ______________
3. total ______________
4. big ______________
5. business ______________
6. come ______________
7. high ______________
8. complete ______________
9. deep ______________
10. honestly ______________

B. Match the words given in the two columns to form collocations.

A	B
1. golden	a. volcano
2. crystal	b. diet
3. active	c. opportunity
4. common	d. friends
5. balanced	e. idea
6. best	f. clear
7. bright	g. sleep
8. deep	h. sense

C. Make sentences using any four collocations you formed in the previous exercise.

____

____

____

____

____

____

____

____

Contextual Usage

D. Complete the sentences with suitable words from the box. All the words are from the story.

lace	crashed	preserve
furniture	spell	scared

1. I was so sleepy that I ____________ in front of all the guests.
2. My parents decided to buy ____________ for our new house.
3. The witch cast a ____________ on the prince and turned him into a frog.
4. A lot of chemicals are used to ____________ food.
5. Bobby was ____________ to enter the dark room.
6. The pink dress is so beautiful because it has ____________ on it.

Grammar in Use

JOINING SENTENCES WITH *WHO*

A. Join the sentences using who.

1. They finally found the boy. The boy was missing for the last 10 days.
2. He is going to the baker. The baker makes the best bread in town.
3. We are reading a book on Rabindranath Tagore. Tagore was a poet.
4. I am fond of watching Mr Bean. Mr Bean is a comic actor.
5. She identified the man. The man had snatched her purse.

PUNCTUATION

B. Rewrite the paragraph using punctuation wherever required.

yuvraj and his brother rajveer wanted to go for a picnic on sunday with their friends rohan nikhil and karan their mother decided to pack sandwiches pastries fruits sweets and a bottle of juice the boys were very happy and thanked their mother for the picnic hamper

Listening and Speaking

Listen carefully to the conversation between a travel agent and a tourist and answer the following questions.

1. At what time of the day did the tourist call the travel agent?

2. Where did the tourist want to go and for how many days?

3. Was the tourist going to travel alone?

4. What was the price of the deal offered by 'Time Travels'?

5. What did the price include?

Pen it Down

Imagine you are Emily. Write a letter to your pen friend describing your experience inside the pyramid.

You may write about the following:

- Were you scared of the life-like structure of the mummy?
- Did you think that the mummy would come alive?
- Did you agree with your uncle that no one was taking care of the pyramids?

17 An Animal's Prayer

Way with Words

Similes

A. Match the sentences in column A with suitable similes in column B.

A	B
1. My mother has long, black hair.	a. as light as feather
2. Even Sima's little brother could carry the bag easily.	b. as busy as a bee
3. The water of the stream is very clear.	c. as black as coal
4. Rajesh has to attend many meetings today.	d. as brave as a lion
5. The man could not see anything without his glasses.	e. as clear as crystal
6. The soldier fought courageously.	f. as blind as a bat

Words Related to Animals

B. Read the clues and solve the crossword puzzle about animals.

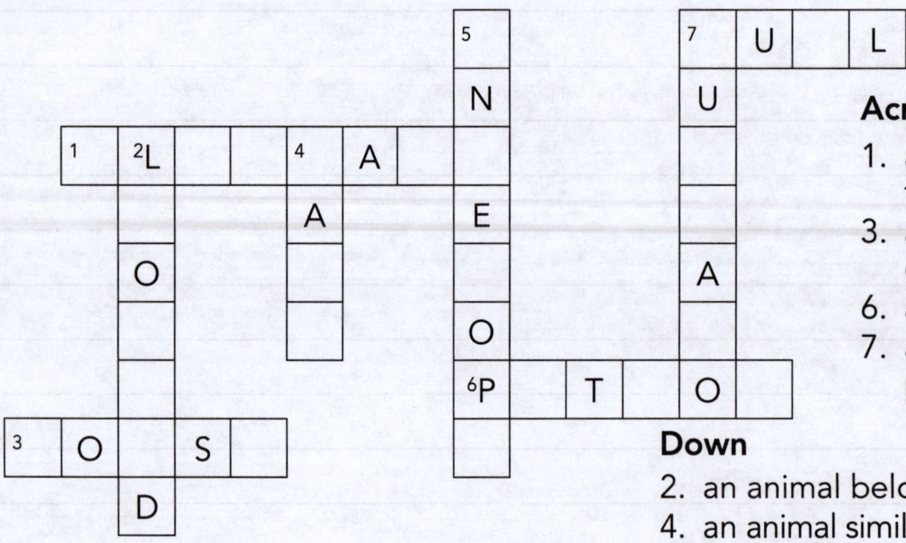

Across

1. an animal with a long trunk
3. an animal used to pull carriages
6. a non-poisonous snake
7. an animal used for ploughing land

Down

2. an animal belonging to the cat family
4. an animal similar to a rabbit but with longer ears
5. a deer-like mammal
7. an animal with curved sharp horns

Grammar in Use

Types of Adverbs

An **adverb** is a word that tells us something more about the action in a sentence by adding meaning to a verb, an adjective or another adverb.
Adverb of manner shows the way an action happens.
Adverb of place tells the location of an action.
Adverb of time shows when or for how long an action took place.

A. Complete the sentences with suitable adverbs from the box.

everywhere	quickly	nearly	already	tomorrow	heavily

1. I have spoken to my teacher ________.
2. He looked for his pet dog ________.
3. Last evening it rained ________.
4. We ________ lost the game.
5. My school will reopen ________.
6. He does all his work ________.

Apostrophe

An **apostrophe** has two functions. It is used to show that something belongs to someone, and for shortening words.
Examples: This is **Reena's** bag. (possession)
I **can't** attend the meeting today. (contraction)

B. Rewrite the sentences using an apostrophe (').

1. We should not touch the pen belonging to Sriya.
____
2. I will not stay in a hostel for boys.
____
3. They picked up the bottle belonging to Ravi and the bag belonging to Ira.
____
4. The sister of Preeti is a college student.
____
5. Radha has not come to school today.
____
6. Sohail and Sumit cannot go to work today because it is raining heavily.
____

7. I am going to the house of my friend.

____

8. The dress belonging to Gargi is very dirty.

____

Listening and Speaking

In groups of five, do a role play to talk about the importance of protecting the environment. You can talk about the following points in the role play:

- a resource which is essential for everyday life
- how it is being misused/wasted
- how wastage can be harmful for the environment
- ways to protect that resource and use it intelligently

Pen it Down

You found a pet dog roaming about in the lane behind your house. You saw the collar and realized that it was either lost or abandoned by the owners. You decided to hand over the dog to an animal shelter. Write the conversation that takes place between you and the manager of the shelter.

You can include the following points:

- the place you found the dog
- how you knew that it was lost
- what you did immediately after you found him
- why you decided to bring it to the animal shelter

You: ____

Manager: ____

You: ____

Manager: ____

You: ____

Manager: ____

____

____

____

Assessment

Comprehension

Text A. Read this Panchatantra story and answer the questions. It is a moral tale about how others try to take advantage of a situation when two people are busy fighting with each other.

A hen built a nest at the bottom of a tree and lived there. One day, she found a paddy field and went to stay there for a while. While she was away, a rabbit found the empty nest and decided to move in.

When the hen returned, she found the rabbit in her nest. She asked him to move out but he refused.

They decided to find someone to settle their fight.

After walking for miles, they reached a river. There, they saw a big tomcat praying. They agreed that the cat would be a good judge.

They told the tomcat what had happened. He sat in silence for a while. Then he said, 'I cannot hear you very well. Please come closer and repeat it.'

They moved closer to explain their problem again. But, before they realized it, the cat struck them with its paws and killed them.

Questions

1. Where did the hen build her nest? (1 mark)

____

2. Where did the hen decide to stay for a while? (1 mark)

____

____

3. What happened while the hen was away? (2 marks)

____

____

4. Why did the hen and the rabbit quarrel? (2 marks)

5. Who did the hen and the rabbit choose as their judge and why? (2 marks)

6. What did this judge ask the hen and rabbit to do and why? (2 marks)

7. *They decided to find someone to settle their quarrel.*

   a) What does the word 'settle' mean in this sentence?

   Copy **one** correct word from the list below.

   solve explain continue answer (1 mark)

   b) The hen and the rabbit found the cat near a ______________.

   Copy **one** word from the list below that correctly completes this sentence:

   river village forest pond (1 mark)

8. According to you, what led the hen and the rabbit to their end? (3 marks)

Text B. Read this passage about the Nepal earthquake of 2015 and answer the questions.

Nepal was hit by a strong earthquake, also called the Gorkha earthquake, on Saturday, 25 April 2015. The earthquake occurred near Barpak, a mountain village near capital Kathmandu. Strong tremors were even felt in Pakistan, India, Bangladesh, Tibet and Bhutan.

The initial tremor was felt just before noon and registered a magnitude of 7.8 on the Richter scale. It was followed by many powerful aftershocks.

The series of earthquakes caused great damage. Thousands of people died while many more were badly injured. Also, many historic buildings, temples and roads got destroyed.

The first earthquake was followed by more than 200 aftershocks and another huge earthquake on 12 May. Experts said that the aftershocks let out the trapped energy under the Earth's surface.

The Himalayan region is seismically active. However, before the 2015 quake, the most recent large earthquake with a magnitude of 6.0 or above took place in 1988.

Questions

1. When did the earthquake hit Nepal? (1 mark)

2. In which areas did it occur? (2 marks)

3. Mention the countries where the tremors were felt. (2 marks)

4. When was the first tremor felt and what was its magnitude? (2 marks)

5. What damage did the earthquake cause in Nepal? (2 marks)

6. What was the view of the experts about this earthquake? (2 marks)

7. *'The initial tremor was felt just before noon...'*

   a) What does 'initial' mean in this sentence?

   Circle **one** correct word from the list below.

   last same new first (1 mark)

   b) Copy one word from the list below that correctly completes this sentence:

   The earthquake is also referred to as the ____________ earthquake.

   Richter Gorkha Barpak Kathmandu (1 mark)

8. According to you, what kind of precautions should one take during an earthquake? Mention any two. (2 marks)

NOTES

NOTES